M000283140

the

OneWord

Journal

the

OneWord

Journal

Your Weekly Journey
for Life-Change

JON GORDON | DAN BRITTON | JIMMY PAGE

WILEY

Published by John Wiley & Sons, Inc., Hoboken, New Jersey.

Published simultaneously in Canada.

For general information on our other products and services or for technical support, please contact our Customer Care Department within the United States at (800) 762-2974, outside the United States at (317) 572-3993 or fax (317) 572-4002.

Wiley also publishes its books in a variety of electronic formats. Some content that appears in print may not be available in electronic formats. For more information about Wiley products, visit our web site at www.wiley.com.

Library of Congress Cataloging-in-Publication Data

Names: Gordon, Jon, 1971- author. | Britton, Dan, author. | Page, Jimmy (James H.), author.
Title: The one word journal : your weekly journey for life-change / Jon Gordon, Dan Britton, Jimmy Page.
Description: Hoboken, New Jersey : Wiley, [2023]
Identifiers: LCCN 2022029606 (print) | LCCN 2022029607 (ebook) | ISBN 9781119907640 (cloth) | ISBN 9781119907657 (ePub) | ISBN 9781119908340 (ePDF)
Subjects: LCSH: Self-actualization (Psychology) | Simplicity.
Classification: LCC BF637.S4 G667 2023 (print) | LCC BF637.S4 (ebook) | DDC 158.1—dc23/eng/20220812
LC record available at https://lccn.loc.gov/2022029606
LC ebook record available at https://lccn.loc.gov/2022029607

COVER DESIGN: PAUL MCCARTHY

SKY10035032_090222

my **One Word**

RESTORE
ADAPT

year

2023

contents

"Tomorrow is the
first blank page
of a 365 page book.
Write a good one."

Brad Paisley

Your *One Word* Journey

Are you ready for one of the most inspirational and transformational experiences of your life? The simple yet powerful practice of focusing on *One Word* for the year brings positive and lasting life-changes. The *One Word* Journey has impacted millions of people, families, companies, and teams. And this little journal may just be the secret to your success.

We often say, "Focus drives progress." That's why we've created this simple journal—to help you stay focused on your *One Word* every day this year. We hope you'll use it to check in with yourself each week and track the insights you've gained, the lessons you've learned, and the progress you've made along the way. This journal is designed to help you remember key moments and milestones, and to get some wins. Expect positive changes to come this year.

Your *One Word* will help you embody the principles you learn and experience true and lasting life-change. And best of all, you will keep track of life-change that happens in every dimension of life: mental, emotional, relational, physical, financial, and spiritual.

Big changes don't happen all at once; they happen over time. Use this journal to keep your *One Word* front and center.

Here's How It Works

Before you begin.

Choose your *One Word* for the year. Need tips on how to choose a word? See Appendix A.

Getting started.

Before diving into your weekly journal, challenge yourself to identify why you chose your *One Word*, the life-changes you hope to see, and who can help you succeed.

Your journey of life-change.

Each week is divided into three main sections: Weekly Focus, Weekly Experience, and Weekly Win. At the beginning of each week, write your *One Word* at the top of the page to keep it front and center. This ensures you don't forget it. Also, write the week you are journeying through. This could be the dates of the week or simply Week 1, Week 2, Week 3, and so on.

Weekly Focus: This section will help you get ready and prepare for the upcoming week. Begin by reading the *One Word* tip for the week that will help you focus on transformation. This insight will help you gain wisdom to implement your *One Word* and take steps toward growth. See Appendix B for a complete list of all 52 weekly tips. As you reflect on this insight, look at all six dimensions of your life and evaluate the areas in which you need your *One Word* the most and why. Then describe how you will put your *One Word* into action this week in specific ways and write down ways you will impact others with your *One Word*.

Weekly Experience: Throughout the week, jot down how your *One Word* is impacting your life. This is where you will capture what you are experiencing, thinking, feeling, and learning. How is your *One Word* shaping and molding you throughout the week? This can be progress made, areas of growth, and who you are becoming. Then capture the many blessings and challenges, successes and struggles, ups and downs of living your word. There are mountaintops and valleys on our *One Word* Journey. Remember, both are a gift from God.

Weekly Win: Before you wrap up your week, pause to identify one win. Write it down, and then also transfer it to the WEEKLY WINS in Appendix C. Small steps lead to big changes. When you track all your small wins on this page, you can look at the year in review and find reasons to celebrate.

Annual review.

At the end of this year, evaluate your *One Word* Journey. Compare this with how you answered the questions when getting started. Celebrate the wins and identify ways to grow during next year's *One Word* Journey. It is invaluable to take time to stop and reflect on your *One Word* Journey.

Let the journey begin.

The *One Word* Journey is not about doing, it's about becoming. Rather than focusing on a particular outcome or result, use this journal to put one foot in front of the other. You'll be on your way to becoming a better person and making a bigger difference in the world.

We believe God has planted seeds of greatness in you. And we are sure this process will cultivate the soil where those seeds can grow and produce a bountiful harvest in your life. Get ready to become the best version of yourself and have the best year of your life. Your *One Word* Journey starts now!

"The journey of a thousand miles begins with a single step."

Lao Tzu

Getting Started

MY ONE WORD

Restore / Adapt

Reasons I chose this word:

I need a season of less striving,
of regrowth, so I can bloom
when ready. I need to be able
to adapt, not fix.

Life-change I hope to experience this year because of my word:

A more positive outlook. Joy.
Rebirth of focus + passion.

Why it is important to others that I live out this word:

Because noone wants a leader/ friend/ wife/ mother who is burnt out & depressed & that's where I'm at.

Ways I will keep my *One Word* front and center:

I got a bracelet to where. I will not take on new responsibilities until my health is better.

Key quotes or scripture verses that emphasize my *One Word*:

Restore unto me the joy of my salvation, and uphold me with a willing spirit.

My "stretch team"—the people who
know me best and are willing to help
encourage me as I make progress:

Jeremy

MI4P Team

_X_ Check here when I've shared my
One Word with them.

Brief description of how they all
responded to what I shared.

Jeremy understands the depth
of my mental struggle & encouraged
me in my word.
Not sure MI4P gets it as much.

"You don't have to see the whole staircase, just take the first step."

Dr. Martin Luther King Jr.

Six Dimensions

Your *One Word* Journey will touch on all six dimensions of your life: physical, mental, emotional, relational, financial, and spiritual. Every dimension is integrated with the others.

Physical

Improvements in your physical health tend to make every other area of life better. Physical health involves your body—things like diet, exercise, and even sleep; it can directly affect your mindset, energy, and enjoyment of life.

Mental

Mental health encompasses the way you think, which leads to how you feel and act. The direction of your life can usually be traced back to the quality of your thoughts. Focusing on your mindset improves the way you experience most of life.

Emotional

Emotional life revolves around how you feel about things, and emotions will influence what you believe and what you do. Identifying and processing feelings like joy, fear, sadness, and anger are part of the emotional journey.

Relational

The quality of your relationships and the level of connection you have with others affects your quality of life. Relationships to consider include family, friends, teammates, coworkers, neighbors, church members, and others with whom you connect with on a consistent basis.

Financial

Money and finances have a way of both blessing our lives and causing us stress. Making progress in your financial life gives you opportunities to live your best life and be a blessing to others.

Spiritual

Belief, faith, and connection to God can change you from the inside out. As author and pastor A. W. Tozer put it, "What comes into our minds when we think about God is the most important thing about us." This dimension gives you a sense of mission and meaning and leads to a satisfying, purposeful, and fulfilling life.

Each week, reflect on how your *One Word* is impacting each dimension, how the dimensions are impacting each other, and which dimension needs to grow the most.

"The object of a New Year is not that we should have a new year. It is that we should have a new soul."

G. K. Chesterton

EXAMPLE ENTRY

WEEK: Jan 1-7, 22   **MY ONE WORD:** Unstoppable

WEEKLY FOCUS
RENEW YOUR FAITH

You are not an accident. You have a purpose. As you start your One Word journey pray for wisdom and insight. Renew your faith and trust in God's bigger plan for your life.

What areas need my *One Word* the most?

- ☑ Physical
- ☐ Emotional
- ☑ Mental
- ☐ Relational
- ☐ Spiritual
- ☐ Financial

Why? I want to change my limiting beliefs that are holding me back. (Mental)

I need a breakthrough on my health goals to lose weight and change my habits to get it done. (Physical)

EXAMPLE ENTRY

I will put my *One Word* into action by...

#1 Paying attention to my thoughts, including doubts and fears.

#2 Changing "can't do" into "can do" statements.

#3 Adding a 15-minute brisk walk every morning.

I will **impact others** with my *One Word* by...

#1 Sharing the changes I'm making with my mindset with my spouse and kids.

#2 Encouraging my inner circle to discover their one word for the year and sharing my one word with them.

WEEKLY EXPERIENCE

Lessons and insights I learned this week living my *One Word*...

#1 I discovered that by paying attention to my patterns of thinking, I can make positive changes.

#2 Negative thoughts make me "stoppable," but by turning them into positive statement, I can change direction and make progress.

#3 By taking small steps consistently, I can make big changes.

#4 I was reminded by the weekly Tip to have unstoppable faith and trust in God.

EXAMPLE ENTRY

The **blessings and challenges** of living my *One Word*...

#1 The biggest blessing has been involving family and coworkers and encouraging them to do one word too.

#2 The biggest challenge was realizing that this process and journey is going to be hard but that it will also be rewarding and bring growth and progress.

WEEKLY WIN

Sticking to my commitments of controlling my thoughts and sharing with my family, friends, and teammates.

WEEK: ___1___   **MY *ONE WORD*:** *Restore*
1/12 - 1/18   *Adapt*

WEEKLY FOCUS
RENEW YOUR FAITH

You are not an accident. You have a purpose. As you start your One Word journey pray for wisdom and insight. Renew your faith and trust in God's bigger plan for your life.

What areas need my *One Word* the most?

☐ Physical   ☐ Emotional

☐ Mental   ☐ Relational

☐ Spiritual   ☐ Financial

Why?_____
_____
_____
_____
_____
_____
_____

I will put my *One Word* into action by:

_____

_____

_____

_____

_____

_____

_____

I will **impact others** with my *One Word* by:

_____

_____

_____

_____

_____

_____

_____

WEEKLY EXPERIENCE

Lessons and insights I learned this week living my *One Word*:

_____

_____

_____

_____

_____

_____

_____

_____

_____

_____

_____

_____

_____

_____

The **blessings and challenges** of living my *One Word*:

_____

_____

_____

_____

_____

_____

_____

_____

WEEKLY WIN

_____

_____

_____

_____

_____

_____

WEEKLY FOCUS
PAY ATTENTION

Intentionality with your One Word will open your eyes and heart to see what you've missed before now. Pay attention to what you see.

What areas need my *One Word* the most?

☐ Physical   ☐ Emotional

☐ Mental   ☐ Relational

☐ Spiritual   ☐ Financial

Why?_____
_____
_____
_____
_____
_____
_____

I will put my *One Word* into action by:

_____

_____

_____

_____

_____

_____

I will **impact others** with my *One Word* by:

_____

_____

_____

_____

_____

_____

_____

WEEKLY EXPERIENCE

Lessons and insights I learned this week living my *One Word*:

_____

_____

_____

_____

_____

_____

_____

_____

_____

_____

_____

_____

_____

_____

_____

The **blessings and challenges** of living my *One Word*:

_____

_____

_____

_____

_____

_____

_____

WEEKLY WIN

_____

_____

_____

_____

_____

WEEKLY FOCUS
EMBRACE THE STRUGGLE

Pain is not meaningless. Every struggle comes with purpose. Apply your One Word to the areas that are bringing you the most stress this week.

What areas need my *One Word* the most?

☐ Physical   ☐ Emotional

☐ Mental   ☐ Relational

☐ Spiritual   ☐ Financial

Why?_____

_____

_____

_____

_____

_____

I will put my *One Word* into action by:

_____

_____

_____

_____

_____

_____

_____

I will **impact others** with my *One Word*
by:

_____

_____

_____

_____

_____

_____

_____

WEEKLY EXPERIENCE

Lessons and insights I learned this week **living my *One Word*:**

_____

_____

_____

_____

_____

_____

_____

_____

_____

_____

_____

_____

_____

_____

_____

The **blessings and challenges** of living my *One Word*:

_____
_____
_____
_____
_____
_____
_____
_____

WEEKLY WIN

_____
_____
_____
_____
_____
_____

WEEKLY FOCUS
CHARACTER COUNTS

How often do you stop to reflect on your character?
Where is it strong? Where do you need to develop?
Look for how your One Word plays a role.

What areas need my *One Word* the most?

☐ Physical   ☐ Emotional

☐ Mental   ☐ Relational

☐ Spiritual   ☐ Financial

Why?_____

_____

_____

_____

_____

_____

_____

I will put my *One Word* **into action by:**

_____

_____

_____

_____

_____

_____

_____

I will **impact others** with my *One Word*
by:

_____

_____

_____

_____

_____

_____

_____

WEEKLY EXPERIENCE

Lessons and insights I learned this week **living my** *One Word*:

_____
_____
_____
_____
_____
_____
_____
_____
_____
_____
_____
_____
_____
_____

The **blessings and challenges** of living my *One Word*:

_____

_____

_____

_____

_____

_____

_____

_____

WEEKLY WIN

_____

_____

_____

_____

_____

_____

WEEKLY FOCUS
MAKE A DIFFERENCE

You were made to make a difference in this world—to leave it a little better than you found it. There is purpose for your life. Your One Word will help reveal it.

What areas need my *One Word* the most?

☐ Physical   ☐ Emotional

☐ Mental   ☐ Relational

☐ Spiritual   ☐ Financial

Why?_____

_____

_____

_____

_____

_____

_____

I will put my *One Word* into action by:

_____

_____

_____

_____

_____

_____

_____

I will impact others with my *One Word* by:

_____

_____

_____

_____

_____

_____

_____

WEEKLY EXPERIENCE

Lessons and insights I learned this
week **living my *One Word*:**

_____

_____

_____

_____

_____

_____

_____

_____

_____

_____

_____

_____

_____

_____

The **blessings and challenges** of living my *One Word*:

_____

_____

_____

_____

_____

_____

_____

WEEKLY WIN

_____

_____

_____

_____

_____

_____

WEEKLY FOCUS
FIND A CAUSE

A cause is something bigger than yourself. Joining a cause can bring passion, purpose, and meaning. Reflect on what causes your One Word is leading you to.

What areas need my *One Word* the most?

☐ Physical   ☐ Emotional

☐ Mental   ☐ Relational

☐ Spiritual   ☐ Financial

Why?_____
_____
_____
_____
_____
_____
_____

I will put my *One Word* **into action by**:

_____

_____

_____

_____

_____

_____

I will **impact others** with my *One Word* by:

_____

_____

_____

_____

_____

_____

WEEKLY EXPERIENCE

Lessons and insights I learned this week living my *One Word*:

_____

_____

_____

_____

_____

_____

_____

_____

_____

_____

_____

_____

_____

_____

The **blessings and challenges** of living my *One Word*:

_____

_____

_____

_____

_____

_____

_____

_____

WEEKLY WIN

_____

_____

_____

_____

_____

WEEK: _____   MY *ONE WORD*: _____

WEEKLY FOCUS
FIGHT DISCOURAGEMENT

Negativity and pessimistic thoughts often bombard us, and they lead to discouragement. Use your One Word to fight this, and instead find encouragement.

What areas need my *One Word* the most?

☐ Physical   ☐ Emotional

☐ Mental   ☐ Relational

☐ Spiritual   ☐ Financial

Why?_____

_____

_____

_____

_____

_____

_____

I will put my *One Word* into action by:

_____

_____

_____

_____

_____

_____

I will **impact others** with my *One Word* by:

_____

_____

_____

_____

_____

_____

_____

WEEKLY EXPERIENCE

Lessons and insights I learned this week **living my *One Word***:

_____

_____

_____

_____

_____

_____

_____

_____

_____

_____

_____

_____

_____

The **blessings and challenges** of
living my *One Word*:

_____
_____
_____
_____
_____
_____
_____
_____
_____

WEEKLY WIN

_____
_____
_____
_____
_____
_____

WEEKLY FOCUS
BELIEVE YOU CAN

A "can do" spirit accomplishes anything. Positivity helps you make forward progress. Consider how your One Word can help you say yes this week.

What areas need my *One Word* the most?

☐ Physical   ☐ Emotional

☐ Mental   ☐ Relational

☐ Spiritual   ☐ Financial

Why?_____

_____

_____

_____

_____

_____

_____

I will put my *One Word* **into action by:**

_____

_____

_____

_____

_____

_____

I will **impact others** with my *One Word* by:

_____

_____

_____

_____

_____

_____

WEEKLY EXPERIENCE

Lessons and insights I learned this week living my *One Word*:

_____

_____

_____

_____

_____

_____

_____

_____

_____

_____

_____

_____

_____

_____

_____

_____

The **blessings and challenges** of living my *One Word*:

_____

_____

_____

_____

_____

_____

_____

_____

WEEKLY WIN

_____

_____

_____

_____

_____

WEEKLY FOCUS
CUT DISTRACTIONS

Notifications, pings, and dings are relentless; they can interrupt us when we're on a roll. How can you remove distractions and focus on your One Word?

What areas need my *One Word* the most?

☐ Physical   ☐ Emotional

☐ Mental   ☐ Relational

☐ Spiritual   ☐ Financial

Why?_____
_____
_____
_____
_____
_____
_____

I will put my *One Word* into action by:

_____

_____

_____

_____

_____

_____

_____

I will **impact others** with my *One Word* by:

_____

_____

_____

_____

_____

_____

_____

WEEKLY EXPERIENCE

Lessons and insights I learned this
week **living my** *One Word*:

_____

_____

_____

_____

_____

_____

_____

_____

_____

_____

_____

_____

_____

_____

_____

The blessings and challenges of living my *One Word*:

_____
_____
_____
_____
_____
_____
_____
_____

WEEKLY WIN

_____
_____
_____
_____
_____
_____

WEEKLY FOCUS
CELEBRATE

Life is full of things worth celebrating. From special occasions to small wins, celebrations make life full. How can your One Word help you celebrate?

What areas need my *One Word* the most?

☐ Physical   ☐ Emotional

☐ Mental   ☐ Relational

☐ Spiritual   ☐ Financial

Why?_____
_____
_____
_____
_____
_____
_____

I will put my *One Word* **into action by:**

_____

_____

_____

_____

_____

_____

_____

I will **impact others** with my *One Word* by:

_____

_____

_____

_____

_____

_____

_____

WEEKLY EXPERIENCE

Lessons and insights I learned this week living my *One Word*:

_____
_____
_____
_____
_____
_____
_____
_____
_____
_____
_____
_____
_____
_____
_____

The **blessings and challenges** of living my *One Word*:

_____

_____

_____

_____

_____

_____

_____

_____

WEEKLY WIN

_____

_____

_____

_____

_____

_____

WEEKLY FOCUS
FIND SMALL WINS

Always build in ways to pause, review your incremental progress, and appreciate how far you've come. Find joy by acknowledging your small wins.

What areas need my *One Word* the most?

- ☐ Physical
- ☐ Emotional
- ☐ Mental
- ☐ Relational
- ☐ Spiritual
- ☐ Financial

Why? _____
_____
_____
_____
_____
_____
_____

I will put my *One Word* into action by:

_____

_____

_____

_____

_____

_____

_____

I will **impact others** with my *One Word* by:

_____

_____

_____

_____

_____

_____

_____

WEEKLY EXPERIENCE

Lessons and insights I learned this week **living my *One Word***:

_____

_____

_____

_____

_____

_____

_____

_____

_____

_____

_____

_____

_____

_____

The blessings and challenges of living my *One Word*:

_____
_____
_____
_____
_____
_____
_____
_____

WEEKLY WIN

_____
_____
_____
_____
_____
_____

WEEKLY FOCUS
CONNECT TO KEEP GOING

Everyone gets discouraged and needs connection to snap out of it. Pick someone in your inner circle and share your One Word progress so far.

What areas need my *One Word* the most?

☐ Physical   ☐ Emotional

☐ Mental   ☐ Relational

☐ Spiritual   ☐ Financial

Why?_____

_____

_____

_____

_____

_____

_____

I will put my *One Word* into action by:

_____

_____

_____

_____

_____

_____

_____

I will **impact others** with my *One Word* by:

_____

_____

_____

_____

_____

_____

_____

WEEKLY EXPERIENCE

Lessons and insights I learned this week **living my *One Word***:

_____

_____

_____

_____

_____

_____

_____

_____

_____

_____

_____

_____

_____

_____

_____

_____

The **blessings and challenges** of living my *One Word*:

_____

_____

_____

_____

_____

_____

_____

_____

WEEKLY WIN

_____

_____

_____

_____

_____

_____

WEEKLY FOCUS
CHECK IN

Don't overestimate the power of your stretch team. They can help you keep your One Word goals on track. Check in with them to share how it's going.

What areas need my *One Word* the most?

☐ Physical   ☐ Emotional

☐ Mental   ☐ Relational

☐ Spiritual   ☐ Financial

Why?_____
_____
_____
_____
_____
_____
_____

I will put my *One Word* **into action by**:

_____
_____
_____
_____
_____
_____
_____

I will **impact others** with my *One Word* by:

_____
_____
_____
_____
_____
_____
_____

WEEKLY EXPERIENCE

Lessons and insights I learned this week living my *One Word*:

_____

_____

_____

_____

_____

_____

_____

_____

_____

_____

_____

_____

_____

The **blessings and challenges** of living my *One Word*:

_____

_____

_____

_____

_____

_____

_____

_____

WEEKLY WIN

_____

_____

_____

_____

_____

_____

WEEKLY FOCUS
MONITOR FOR BURNOUT

A fast pace can lead to burnout and discouragement. Your One Word will bring you life. In what areas are you feeling burned out? Make a plan to go slower.

What areas need my *One Word* the most?

- ☐ Physical
- ☐ Emotional
- ☐ Mental
- ☐ Relational
- ☐ Spiritual
- ☐ Financial

Why?_____

_____

_____

_____

_____

_____

I will put my *One Word* into action by:

_____

_____

_____

_____

_____

_____

_____

I will **impact others** with my *One Word* by:

_____

_____

_____

_____

_____

_____

_____

WEEKLY EXPERIENCE

Lessons and insights I learned this week living my *One Word*:

_____

_____

_____

_____

_____

_____

_____

_____

_____

_____

_____

_____

_____

_____

The **blessings and challenges** of living my *One Word*:

_____

_____

_____

_____

_____

_____

_____

_____

WEEKLY WIN

_____

_____

_____

_____

_____

WEEKLY FOCUS
REMEMBER YOUR "WHY"

Why did you choose your One Word? What motivated you to dive into this journey? Remember your "why" to find momentum to keep going.

What areas need my *One Word* the most?

☐ Physical   ☐ Emotional

☐ Mental   ☐ Relational

☐ Spiritual   ☐ Financial

Why?_____
_____
_____
_____
_____
_____
_____

I will put my *One Word* into action by:

_____

_____

_____

_____

_____

_____

_____

I will **impact others** with my *One Word* by:

_____

_____

_____

_____

_____

_____

_____

WEEKLY EXPERIENCE

Lessons and insights I learned this
week **living my *One Word***:

_____

_____

_____

_____

_____

_____

_____

_____

_____

_____

_____

_____

_____

_____

The **blessings and challenges** of living my *One Word*:

_____

_____

_____

_____

_____

_____

_____

_____

WEEKLY WIN

_____

_____

_____

_____

_____

_____

WEEKLY FOCUS
KEEP IT FRESH

Find someone new with whom to share your One Word, someone who hasn't heard it before. Tell them why you chose it and the impact it's made on your life so far.

What areas need my *One Word* the most?

☐ Physical   ☐ Emotional

☐ Mental   ☐ Relational

☐ Spiritual   ☐ Financial

Why?_____
_____
_____
_____
_____
_____
_____

I will put my *One Word* **into action by:**

_____

_____

_____

_____

_____

_____

_____

I will **impact others** with my *One Word* by:

_____

_____

_____

_____

_____

_____

_____

WEEKLY EXPERIENCE

Lessons and insights I learned this week living my *One Word*:

_____

_____

_____

_____

_____

_____

_____

_____

_____

_____

_____

_____

_____

_____

The **blessings and challenges** of living my *One Word*:

_____

_____

_____

_____

_____

_____

_____

_____

WEEKLY WIN

_____

_____

_____

_____

_____

WEEKLY FOCUS
DEFINE SUCCESS

Some say success is winning over losing. Some say it's completion. Some say it's doing the right things consistently over time. How do you define it?

What areas need my *One Word* the most?

☐ Physical   ☐ Emotional

☐ Mental   ☐ Relational

☐ Spiritual   ☐ Financial

Why?_____

_____

_____

_____

_____

_____

I will put my *One Word* into action by:

_____

_____

_____

_____

_____

_____

_____

I will **impact others** with my *One Word* by:

_____

_____

_____

_____

_____

_____

_____

WEEKLY EXPERIENCE

Lessons and insights I learned this
week living my *One Word*:

_____
_____
_____
_____
_____
_____
_____
_____
_____
_____
_____
_____
_____
_____

The **blessings and challenges** of living my *One Word*:

_____

_____

_____

_____

_____

_____

_____

_____

WEEKLY WIN

_____

_____

_____

_____

_____

_____

WEEKLY FOCUS
BE CONSISTENT

*Starts and stops threaten to derail progress.
Doing the little things every day to pursue your
One Word will create the results you want.*

What areas need my *One Word* the most?

☐ Physical   ☐ Emotional

☐ Mental   ☐ Relational

☐ Spiritual   ☐ Financial

Why?_____
_____
_____
_____
_____
_____
_____

I will put my *One Word* **into action by:**

_____

_____

_____

_____

_____

_____

I will **impact others** with my *One Word* by:

_____

_____

_____

_____

_____

_____

WEEKLY EXPERIENCE

Lessons and insights I learned this
week **living my *One Word*:**

_____
_____
_____
_____
_____
_____
_____
_____
_____
_____
_____
_____
_____
_____
_____
_____

The **blessings and challenges** of living my *One Word*:

_____

_____

_____

_____

_____

_____

_____

WEEKLY WIN

_____

_____

_____

_____

_____

_____

WEEKLY FOCUS
TAKE ACTION

It's one thing to think up a plan; it's another to take action. Your One Word Journey requires action. Don't just think this week—do.

What areas need my *One Word* the most?

☐ Physical   ☐ Emotional

☐ Mental   ☐ Relational

☐ Spiritual   ☐ Financial

Why?_____

_____

_____

_____

_____

_____

_____

I will put my *One Word* into action by:

_____

_____

_____

_____

_____

_____

_____

I will **impact others** with my *One Word* by:

_____

_____

_____

_____

_____

_____

_____

WEEKLY EXPERIENCE

Lessons and insights I learned this
week **living my *One Word***:

_____

_____

_____

_____

_____

_____

_____

_____

_____

_____

_____

_____

_____

_____

_____

The **blessings and challenges** of living my *One Word*:

_____

_____

_____

_____

_____

_____

_____

WEEKLY WIN

_____

_____

_____

_____

_____

WEEK: _____   MY *ONE WORD*: _____

WEEKLY FOCUS
FRONT AND CENTER

What reminder systems work for you and help you keep things front and center each morning? Set up a way for your One Word to be front and center.

What areas need my *One Word* the most?

☐ Physical   ☐ Emotional

☐ Mental   ☐ Relational

☐ Spiritual   ☐ Financial

Why?_____
_____
_____
_____
_____
_____
_____

I will put my *One Word* **into action by:**

_____

_____

_____

_____

_____

_____

I will **impact others** with my *One Word* by:

_____

_____

_____

_____

_____

_____

WEEKLY EXPERIENCE

Lessons and insights I learned this
week **living my *One Word***:

_____

_____

_____

_____

_____

_____

_____

_____

_____

_____

_____

_____

_____

_____

_____

_____

The **blessings and challenges** of
living my *One Word*:

_____

_____

_____

_____

_____

_____

_____

WEEKLY WIN

_____

_____

_____

_____

_____

_____

WEEKLY FOCUS
FIND THE INCH

"Inch by inch, life's a cinch. Yard by yard, life's hard." In what ways have you made inches of progress in your One Word Journey so far? Find and celebrate.

What areas need my *One Word* the most?

☐ Physical   ☐ Emotional

☐ Mental   ☐ Relational

☐ Spiritual   ☐ Financial

Why?_____
_____
_____
_____
_____
_____
_____

I will put my *One Word* into action by:

_____

_____

_____

_____

_____

_____

I will **impact others** with my *One Word* by:

_____

_____

_____

_____

_____

_____

WEEKLY EXPERIENCE

Lessons and insights I learned this week **living my *One Word***:

_____

_____

_____

_____

_____

_____

_____

_____

_____

_____

_____

_____

_____

_____

_____

The **blessings and challenges** of living my *One Word*:

_____

_____

_____

_____

_____

_____

_____

_____

WEEKLY WIN

_____

_____

_____

_____

_____

WEEKLY FOCUS
FOCUS ON NOW

There's nothing worse than feeling stuck, like nothing positive is happening. But sometimes you're looking too far ahead. Focus on what's happening today.

What areas need my *One Word* the most?

☐ Physical   ☐ Emotional

☐ Mental   ☐ Relational

☐ Spiritual   ☐ Financial

Why?_____

_____

_____

_____

_____

_____

_____

I will put my *One Word* into action by:

_____

_____

_____

_____

_____

_____

I will **impact others** with my *One Word* by:

_____

_____

_____

_____

_____

_____

WEEKLY EXPERIENCE

Lessons and insights I learned this week **living my *One Word***:

_____

_____

_____

_____

_____

_____

_____

_____

_____

_____

_____

_____

_____

_____

_____

The **blessings and challenges** of living my *One Word*:

_____

_____

_____

_____

_____

_____

_____

_____

WEEKLY WIN

_____

_____

_____

_____

_____

_____

WEEKLY FOCUS
STEP EACH STEP

Temptation tells us to skip steps on the One Word Journey and bypass challenges and hard work. But to get the results you want, don't miss a step.

What areas need my *One Word* the most?

☐ Physical   ☐ Emotional

☐ Mental   ☐ Relational

☐ Spiritual   ☐ Financial

Why?_____

_____

_____

_____

_____

_____

_____

I will put my *One Word* into action by:

_____

_____

_____

_____

_____

_____

_____

I will impact others with my *One Word* by:

_____

_____

_____

_____

_____

_____

_____

WEEKLY EXPERIENCE

Lessons and insights I learned this week living my *One Word*:

_____

_____

_____

_____

_____

_____

_____

_____

_____

_____

_____

_____

_____

_____

The **blessings and challenges** of living my *One Word*:

_____

_____

_____

_____

_____

_____

_____

_____

WEEKLY WIN

_____

_____

_____

_____

_____

_____

WEEKLY FOCUS
LOOK FOR OPPORTUNITIES

If you pray for patience, God won't automatically make you patient; He will give you opportunities to grow. Consider the opportunities before you this week.

What areas need my _One Word_ the most?

☐ Physical   ☐ Emotional

☐ Mental   ☐ Relational

☐ Spiritual   ☐ Financial

Why?_____

_____

_____

_____

_____

_____

I will put my *One Word* **into action by**:

_____

_____

_____

_____

_____

_____

_____

I will **impact others** with my *One Word* by:

_____

_____

_____

_____

_____

_____

_____

WEEKLY EXPERIENCE

Lessons and insights I learned this week living my *One Word*:

_____

_____

_____

_____

_____

_____

_____

_____

_____

_____

_____

_____

_____

_____

The **blessings and challenges** of living my *One Word*:

_____

_____

_____

_____

_____

_____

_____

_____

WEEKLY WIN

_____

_____

_____

_____

_____

_____

WEEKLY FOCUS
PROCESS OVER PROBLEMS

Life brings potholes and speed bumps, but progress is a process. Let your One Word help you focus on the person you are becoming over the problems.

What areas need my *One Word* the most?

☐ Physical   ☐ Emotional

☐ Mental   ☐ Relational

☐ Spiritual   ☐ Financial

Why?_____

_____

_____

_____

_____

_____

I will put my *One Word* **into action by:**

_____

_____

_____

_____

_____

_____

I will **impact others** with my *One Word* by:

_____

_____

_____

_____

_____

_____

WEEKLY EXPERIENCE

Lessons and insights I learned this
week **living my *One Word*:**

_____

_____

_____

_____

_____

_____

_____

_____

_____

_____

_____

_____

_____

The blessings and challenges of
living my *One Word*:

_____

_____

_____

_____

_____

_____

_____

_____

WEEKLY WIN

_____

_____

_____

_____

_____

_____

WEEKLY FOCUS
DO NOT DISTURB

Without intentionally setting aside time to focus on your One Word Journey, you will miss it. Set aside time where you can't be disturbed so you can truly reflect.

What areas need my *One Word* the most?

☐ Physical   ☐ Emotional

☐ Mental   ☐ Relational

☐ Spiritual   ☐ Financial

Why? _____
_____
_____
_____
_____
_____
_____

I will put my *One Word* **into action by:**

_____

_____

_____

_____

_____

_____

_____

I will **impact others** with my *One Word* by:

_____

_____

_____

_____

_____

_____

_____

WEEKLY EXPERIENCE

Lessons and insights I learned this week living my *One Word*:

_____

_____

_____

_____

_____

_____

_____

_____

_____

_____

_____

_____

_____

_____

The **blessings and challenges** of living my *One Word*:

_____

_____

_____

_____

_____

_____

_____

_____

WEEKLY WIN

_____

_____

_____

_____

_____

WEEKLY FOCUS
KEEP GOING

Demand and perseverance on the front-end leads to big-time payoffs in the end. If you're in the middle, don't quit. Let your One Word keep you focused.

What areas need my *One Word* the most?

☐ Physical   ☐ Emotional

☐ Mental   ☐ Relational

☐ Spiritual   ☐ Financial

Why?_____

_____

_____

_____

_____

_____

I will put my *One Word* into action by:

_____

_____

_____

_____

_____

_____

_____

I will **impact others** with my *One Word* by:

_____

_____

_____

_____

_____

_____

_____

_____

WEEKLY EXPERIENCE

Lessons and insights I learned this
week living my *One Word*:

_____

_____

_____

_____

_____

_____

_____

_____

_____

_____

_____

_____

_____

_____

_____

_____

The **blessings and challenges** of living my *One Word*:

_____
_____
_____
_____
_____
_____
_____
_____

WEEKLY WIN

_____
_____
_____
_____
_____
_____

WEEK: _____   MY *ONE WORD*: _____

WEEKLY FOCUS
EXPECT THE UNEXPECTED

Don't be someone who says, "I didn't see that coming." Expect the unexpected. Even if you have an idea about how One Word will turn out, be open to surprise.

What areas need my *One Word* the most?

☐ Physical   ☐ Emotional

☐ Mental   ☐ Relational

☐ Spiritual   ☐ Financial

Why?_____
_____
_____
_____
_____
_____

I will put my *One Word* **into action by**:

_____

_____

_____

_____

_____

_____

_____

I will **impact others** with my *One Word* by:

_____

_____

_____

_____

_____

_____

_____

WEEKLY EXPERIENCE

Lessons and insights I learned this week living my *One Word*:

_____

_____

_____

_____

_____

_____

_____

_____

_____

_____

_____

_____

_____

_____

The **blessings and challenges** of living my *One Word*:

_____
_____
_____
_____
_____
_____
_____
_____
_____

WEEKLY WIN

_____
_____
_____
_____
_____
_____

WEEK: _____   MY *ONE WORD*: _____

WEEKLY FOCUS
IN PLAIN SIGHT

"Out of sight, out of mind." It's a common phrase, but it's true. Remember your One Word this week and put it in plain sight. Make sure you won't miss it.

What areas need my *One Word* the most?

☐ Physical   ☐ Emotional

☐ Mental   ☐ Relational

☐ Spiritual   ☐ Financial

Why?_____

_____

_____

_____

_____

_____

_____

I will put my *One Word* into **action by**:

_____

_____

_____

_____

_____

_____

I will **impact others** with my *One Word*
by:

_____

_____

_____

_____

_____

_____

WEEKLY EXPERIENCE

Lessons and insights I learned this
week **living my *One Word*:**

_____

_____

_____

_____

_____

_____

_____

_____

_____

_____

_____

_____

_____

_____

_____

The blessings and challenges of living my *One Word*:

_____

_____

_____

_____

_____

_____

_____

_____

WEEKLY WIN

_____

_____

_____

_____

_____

WEEK: _____ **MY *ONE WORD*:** _____

WEEKLY FOCUS
PRESS PAUSE

Are you going so fast that you're missing what matters most to you? It's time to press pause and slow down. Be present and reflect over your One Word.

What areas need my *One Word* the most?

☐ Physical   ☐ Emotional

☐ Mental   ☐ Relational

☐ Spiritual   ☐ Financial

Why?_____

_____

_____

_____

_____

_____

I will put my *One Word* into action by:

_____

_____

_____

_____

_____

_____

_____

I will **impact others** with my *One Word* by:

_____

_____

_____

_____

_____

_____

_____

WEEKLY EXPERIENCE

Lessons and insights I learned this week living my *One Word*:

_____

_____

_____

_____

_____

_____

_____

_____

_____

_____

_____

_____

_____

The **blessings and challenges** of living my *One Word*:

_____

_____

_____

_____

_____

_____

_____

_____

WEEKLY WIN

_____

_____

_____

_____

_____

_____

WEEK: _____ MY *ONE WORD*: _____

WEEKLY FOCUS
SLOW DOWN

Are you addicted to busyness? Did you know it will distract you and put you on overdrive? What's one less thing you can do this week?

What areas need my *One Word* the most?

☐ Physical   ☐ Emotional

☐ Mental   ☐ Relational

☐ Spiritual   ☐ Financial

Why?_____
_____
_____
_____
_____
_____
_____

I will put my *One Word* into action by:

_____

_____

_____

_____

_____

_____

I will **impact others** with my *One Word* by:

_____

_____

_____

_____

_____

_____

_____

WEEKLY EXPERIENCE

Lessons and insights I learned this week **living my *One Word*:**

_____

_____

_____

_____

_____

_____

_____

_____

_____

_____

_____

_____

_____

_____

_____

The **blessings and challenges** of living my *One Word*:

_____
_____
_____
_____
_____
_____
_____
_____
_____

WEEKLY WIN

_____
_____
_____
_____
_____
_____

WEEKLY FOCUS
BE PRESENT

Your journey has a beginning and an end. It's good to remember the goal. But don't forget to be present. How is your One Word impacting your life right now?

What areas need my *One Word* the most?

☐ Physical   ☐ Emotional

☐ Mental   ☐ Relational

☐ Spiritual   ☐ Financial

Why?_____

_____

_____

_____

_____

_____

I will put my *One Word* into action by:

_____

_____

_____

_____

_____

_____

_____

I will **impact others** with my *One Word* by:

_____

_____

_____

_____

_____

_____

_____

WEEKLY EXPERIENCE

Lessons and insights I learned this
week living my *One Word*:

_____
_____
_____
_____
_____
_____
_____
_____
_____
_____
_____
_____
_____
_____

The **blessings and challenges** of living my *One Word*:

_____

_____

_____

_____

_____

_____

_____

_____

WEEKLY WIN

_____

_____

_____

_____

_____

_____

WEEK: _____   MY *ONE WORD*: _____

WEEKLY FOCUS
SHARE WITH OTHERS

Telling others about your One Word Journey will bless them and reinvigorate you. Sharing benefits others and creates momentum. Share this week.

What areas need my *One Word* the most?

☐ Physical   ☐ Emotional

☐ Mental   ☐ Relational

☐ Spiritual   ☐ Financial

Why?_____

_____

_____

_____

_____

_____

I will put my *One Word* into **action by:**

_____

_____

_____

_____

_____

_____

_____

I will **impact others** with my *One Word*
by:

_____

_____

_____

_____

_____

_____

_____

WEEKLY EXPERIENCE

Lessons and insights I learned this
week **living my _One Word_**:

_____

_____

_____

_____

_____

_____

_____

_____

_____

_____

_____

_____

_____

The blessings and challenges of living my *One Word*:

_____

_____

_____

_____

_____

_____

_____

WEEKLY WIN

_____

_____

_____

_____

_____

_____

WEEKLY FOCUS
BETTER TOGETHER

One Word doesn't benefit only you; it can also benefit the groups you're in. How can your family, friends, team, and other groups benefit from your One Word?

What areas need my *One Word* the most?

☐ Physical   ☐ Emotional

☐ Mental   ☐ Relational

☐ Spiritual   ☐ Financial

Why?_____
_____
_____
_____
_____
_____

I will put my *One Word* into action by:

_____

_____

_____

_____

_____

_____

_____

I will **impact others** with my *One Word* by:

_____

_____

_____

_____

_____

_____

_____

WEEKLY EXPERIENCE

Lessons and insights I learned this week **living my** *One Word*:

_____

_____

_____

_____

_____

_____

_____

_____

_____

_____

_____

_____

_____

_____

_____

The **blessings and challenges** of living my *One Word*:

_____

_____

_____

_____

_____

_____

_____

_____

WEEKLY WIN

_____

_____

_____

_____

_____

_____

WEEKLY FOCUS
BUILD CHEMISTRY

Build unity and trust with teams, companies, and families by choosing a One Word together. It will become a rallying cry and keep you focused on your mission.

What areas need my *One Word* the most?

☐ Physical   ☐ Emotional

☐ Mental   ☐ Relational

☐ Spiritual   ☐ Financial

Why?_____

_____

_____

_____

_____

_____

I will put my *One Word* **into action by:**

_____

_____

_____

_____

_____

_____

_____

I will **impact others** with my *One Word* by:

_____

_____

_____

_____

_____

_____

_____

WEEKLY EXPERIENCE

Lessons and insights I learned this
week **living my *One Word***:

_____

_____

_____

_____

_____

_____

_____

_____

_____

_____

_____

_____

_____

_____

The **blessings and challenges** of living my *One Word*:

_____

_____

_____

_____

_____

_____

_____

_____

WEEKLY WIN

_____

_____

_____

_____

_____

_____

WEEKLY FOCUS
TALK ABOUT IT

Conversations about your One Word will both help you and help others. Share your big wins. Share your small wins. Ask for help. Talk about it.

What areas need my *One Word* the most?

☐ Physical   ☐ Emotional

☐ Mental   ☐ Relational

☐ Spiritual   ☐ Financial

Why?_____
_____
_____
_____
_____
_____

I will put my *One Word* **into action by:**

_____
_____
_____
_____
_____
_____
_____

I will **impact others** with my *One Word* by:

_____
_____
_____
_____
_____
_____
_____

WEEKLY EXPERIENCE

Lessons and insights I learned this
week living my *One Word*:

_____
_____
_____
_____
_____
_____
_____
_____
_____
_____
_____
_____
_____
_____
_____
_____

The **blessings and challenges** of living my *One Word*:

_____

_____

_____

_____

_____

_____

_____

_____

WEEKLY WIN

_____

_____

_____

_____

_____

_____

WEEKLY FOCUS
BLESS OTHERS

As we become our best, we are better to others. Let One Word change you and make you more focused on serving and blessing others in your life.

What areas need my *One Word* the most?

☐ Physical   ☐ Emotional

☐ Mental   ☐ Relational

☐ Spiritual   ☐ Financial

Why?_____

_____

_____

_____

_____

_____

I will put my *One Word* into action by:

_____

_____

_____

_____

_____

_____

_____

I will **impact others** with my *One Word* by:

_____

_____

_____

_____

_____

_____

_____

WEEKLY EXPERIENCE

Lessons and insights I learned this
week **living my *One Word*:**

_____

_____

_____

_____

_____

_____

_____

_____

_____

_____

_____

_____

_____

_____

The **blessings and challenges** of living my *One Word*:

_____
_____
_____
_____
_____
_____
_____
_____

WEEKLY WIN

_____
_____
_____
_____
_____
_____

WEEKLY FOCUS
DISCOVER

Do you feel like your One Word picked you, rather than you picked it? A lot of people do. There's a reason why it's for you this year. Discover it.

What areas need my *One Word* the most?

☐ Physical   ☐ Emotional

☐ Mental   ☐ Relational

☐ Spiritual   ☐ Financial

Why?_____
_____
_____
_____
_____
_____
_____

I will put my *One Word* **into action by**:

_____

_____

_____

_____

_____

_____

_____

I will **impact others** with my *One Word* by:

_____

_____

_____

_____

_____

_____

_____

WEEKLY EXPERIENCE

Lessons and insights I learned this
week **living my** *One Word*:

_____
_____
_____
_____
_____
_____
_____
_____
_____
_____
_____
_____
_____
_____
_____

The **blessings and challenges** of living my *One Word*:

_____

_____

_____

_____

_____

_____

_____

_____

WEEKLY WIN

_____

_____

_____

_____

_____

WEEKLY FOCUS
PROGRESS NOT PERFECTION

Too many people feel like there is a perfect world, and the One Word Journey will be perfect. There is no such thing. There will be hills and valleys. Pursue progress, not perfection.

What areas need my *One Word* the most?

☐ Physical   ☐ Emotional

☐ Mental   ☐ Relational

☐ Spiritual   ☐ Financial

Why?_____

_____

_____

_____

_____

_____

_____

I will put my *One Word* into action by:

_____

_____

_____

_____

_____

_____

_____

I will **impact others** with my *One Word* by:

_____

_____

_____

_____

_____

_____

_____

WEEKLY EXPERIENCE

Lessons and insights I learned this
week **living my *One Word*:**

_____
_____
_____
_____
_____
_____
_____
_____
_____
_____
_____
_____
_____
_____
_____

The **blessings and challenges** of living my *One Word*:

_____
_____
_____
_____
_____
_____
_____
_____

WEEKLY WIN

_____
_____
_____
_____
_____
_____

WEEKLY FOCUS
GROW VERSUS CONQUER

Everybody loves winning, but One Word isn't about winning or conquering. Take inventory on how your One Word is helping you grow through success and failure.

What areas need my *One Word* the most?

☐ Physical   ☐ Emotional

☐ Mental   ☐ Relational

☐ Spiritual   ☐ Financial

Why?_____
_____
_____
_____
_____
_____

I will put my *One Word* into action by:

_____

_____

_____

_____

_____

_____

I will **impact others** with my *One Word*
by:

_____

_____

_____

_____

_____

_____

WEEKLY EXPERIENCE

Lessons and insights I learned this week living my *One Word*:

_____

_____

_____

_____

_____

_____

_____

_____

_____

_____

_____

_____

_____

_____

The **blessings and challenges** of living my *One Word*:

_____

_____

_____

_____

_____

_____

_____

_____

WEEKLY WIN

_____

_____

_____

_____

_____

WEEK: _____ MY *ONE WORD*: _____

WEEKLY FOCUS
DON'T LOOK BACK

Disappointment and fatigue may cause you to want a "redo." Don't give in. Keep moving forward and trust your process. Take steps forward, not back.

What areas need my *One Word* the most?

☐ Physical   ☐ Emotional

☐ Mental   ☐ Relational

☐ Spiritual   ☐ Financial

Why?_____

_____

_____

_____

_____

_____

_____

I will put my *One Word* into action by:

_____

_____

_____

_____

_____

_____

I will **impact others** with my *One Word* by:

_____

_____

_____

_____

_____

_____

WEEKLY EXPERIENCE

Lessons and insights I learned this week **living my _One Word_**:

_____

_____

_____

_____

_____

_____

_____

_____

_____

_____

_____

_____

_____

_____

_____

The **blessings and challenges** of living my *One Word*:

_____

_____

_____

_____

_____

_____

_____

_____

WEEKLY WIN

_____

_____

_____

_____

_____

_____

WEEKLY FOCUS
DON'T COMPARE

Your One Word Journey is unique to you. Don't compare it with others, and don't compare it with past years. Focus on the present year, on today.

What areas need my *One Word* the most?

☐ Physical   ☐ Emotional

☐ Mental   ☐ Relational

☐ Spiritual   ☐ Financial

Why?_____

_____

_____

_____

_____

_____

I will put my *One Word* into action by:

_____

_____

_____

_____

_____

_____

I will **impact others** with my *One Word* by:

_____

_____

_____

_____

_____

_____

WEEKLY EXPERIENCE

Lessons and insights I learned this week living my *One Word*:

_____

_____

_____

_____

_____

_____

_____

_____

_____

_____

_____

_____

_____

_____

The blessings and challenges of living my *One Word*:

_____

_____

_____

_____

_____

_____

_____

_____

WEEKLY WIN

_____

_____

_____

_____

_____

_____

WEEKLY FOCUS
MAKE A DIFFERENCE

When your One Word infiltrates every area of your life, you'll find that the people around you will benefit too. Let your One Word help those you serve.

What areas need my *One Word* the most?

☐ Physical   ☐ Emotional

☐ Mental   ☐ Relational

☐ Spiritual   ☐ Financial

Why?_____
_____
_____
_____
_____
_____
_____

I will put my *One Word* **into action by**:

_____

_____

_____

_____

_____

_____

_____

I will **impact others** with my *One Word* by:

_____

_____

_____

_____

_____

_____

_____

WEEKLY EXPERIENCE

Lessons and insights I learned this
week living my *One Word*:

_____

_____

_____

_____

_____

_____

_____

_____

_____

_____

_____

_____

_____

_____

The **blessings and challenges** of living my *One Word*:

_____
_____
_____
_____
_____
_____
_____
_____

WEEKLY WIN

_____
_____
_____
_____
_____

WEEKLY FOCUS
ENJOY THE JOURNEY

One Word is meant to be fun. It's meant to be life-changing. While it may get hard and challenging at some points, find the positives and enjoy it.

What areas need my *One Word* the most?

☐ Physical   ☐ Emotional

☐ Mental   ☐ Relational

☐ Spiritual   ☐ Financial

Why?_____

_____

_____

_____

_____

_____

_____

I will put my *One Word* **into action by**:

_____

_____

_____

_____

_____

_____

_____

I will **impact others** with my *One Word* by:

_____

_____

_____

_____

_____

_____

_____

WEEKLY EXPERIENCE

Lessons and insights I learned this week **living my *One Word*:**

_____

_____

_____

_____

_____

_____

_____

_____

_____

_____

_____

_____

_____

_____

The **blessings and challenges** of living my *One Word*:

_____
_____
_____
_____
_____
_____
_____
_____

WEEKLY WIN

_____
_____
_____
_____
_____
_____

WEEKLY FOCUS
HIDDEN TREASURES

You may be surprised at the ways One Word is showing up. It's normal if you thought you'd see change in one area, only to find it somewhere else. Keep going.

What areas need my *One Word* the most?

☐ Physical   ☐ Emotional

☐ Mental   ☐ Relational

☐ Spiritual   ☐ Financial

Why?_____

_____

_____

_____

_____

_____

_____

I will put my *One Word* **into action by:**

_____

_____

_____

_____

_____

_____

_____

I will **impact others** with my *One Word* by:

_____

_____

_____

_____

_____

_____

_____

WEEKLY EXPERIENCE

Lessons and insights I learned this week **living my _One Word_**:

_____

_____

_____

_____

_____

_____

_____

_____

_____

_____

_____

_____

_____

_____

The **blessings and challenges** of living my *One Word*:

_____

_____

_____

_____

_____

_____

_____

_____

WEEKLY WIN

_____

_____

_____

_____

_____

WEEK: _____   MY *ONE WORD*: _____

WEEKLY FOCUS
KEEP IT SIMPLE

One Word is designed to be a simple way to experience life transformation. It's not meant to be complicated, and it doesn't need to be. Resist complexity.

What areas need my *One Word* the most?

☐ Physical   ☐ Emotional

☐ Mental   ☐ Relational

☐ Spiritual   ☐ Financial

Why?_____

_____

_____

_____

_____

_____

_____

I will put my *One Word* **into action by:**

_____
_____
_____
_____
_____
_____

I will **impact others** with my *One Word* by:

_____
_____
_____
_____
_____
_____

WEEKLY EXPERIENCE

Lessons and insights I learned this week **living my *One Word*:**

_____

_____

_____

_____

_____

_____

_____

_____

_____

_____

_____

_____

_____

_____

The **blessings and challenges** of living my *One Word*:

_____

_____

_____

_____

_____

_____

_____

WEEKLY WIN

_____

_____

_____

_____

_____

_____

WEEKLY FOCUS
SAY NO

Boundaries: Do you have them? Your One Word is a guide for your year, and to follow it you'll likely need to say no so you can stay on track. Practice it. Boundaries are worth it.

What areas need my *One Word* the most?

☐ Physical   ☐ Emotional

☐ Mental   ☐ Relational

☐ Spiritual   ☐ Financial

Why?_____

_____

_____

_____

_____

_____

_____

I will put my *One Word* **into action by:**

_____

_____

_____

_____

_____

_____

_____

I will **impact others** with my *One Word* by:

_____

_____

_____

_____

_____

_____

_____

WEEKLY EXPERIENCE

Lessons and insights I learned this week **living my *One Word*:**

_____

_____

_____

_____

_____

_____

_____

_____

_____

_____

_____

_____

_____

_____

_____

_____

The **blessings and challenges** of living my *One Word*:

_____

_____

_____

_____

_____

_____

_____

_____

WEEKLY WIN

_____

_____

_____

_____

_____

_____

WEEK: _____   MY *ONE WORD*: _____

WEEKLY FOCUS
THE ANSWER

One Word is a guiding light for your year. Faced with decisions and trying to discern which way to go? Consider how your One Word may be leading to your answer.

What areas need my *One Word* the most?

☐ Physical   ☐ Emotional

☐ Mental   ☐ Relational

☐ Spiritual   ☐ Financial

Why?_____
_____
_____
_____
_____
_____

I will put my *One Word* **into action by:**

_____

_____

_____

_____

_____

_____

_____

I will **impact others** with my *One Word* by:

_____

_____

_____

_____

_____

_____

_____

WEEKLY EXPERIENCE

Lessons and insights I learned this
week living my *One Word*:

_____
_____
_____
_____
_____
_____
_____
_____
_____
_____
_____
_____
_____
_____
_____

The **blessings and challenges** of living my *One Word*:

_____

_____

_____

_____

_____

_____

_____

_____

WEEKLY WIN

_____

_____

_____

_____

_____

_____

WEEKLY FOCUS
PUSH YOURSELF

The One Word Journey won't be comfortable; change creates tension, but tension leads to growth. In what ways are you challenged to push yourself to become a better you?

What areas need my *One Word* the most?

☐ Physical   ☐ Emotional

☐ Mental   ☐ Relational

☐ Spiritual   ☐ Financial

Why?_____
_____
_____
_____
_____
_____
_____

I will put my *One Word* into action by:

_____

_____

_____

_____

_____

_____

_____

I will **impact others** with my *One Word* by:

_____

_____

_____

_____

_____

_____

_____

WEEKLY EXPERIENCE

Lessons and insights I learned this week living my *One Word*:

_____

_____

_____

_____

_____

_____

_____

_____

_____

_____

_____

_____

_____

_____

_____

The **blessings and challenges** of living my *One Word*:

_____

_____

_____

_____

_____

_____

_____

_____

WEEKLY WIN

_____

_____

_____

_____

_____

_____

WEEK: _____   **MY *ONE WORD*:** _____

WEEKLY FOCUS
SAY YES

How does fear hold you back? What dreams have yet to become a reality? Consider how your One Word is leading you to say yes to what's previously been a no.

What areas need my *One Word* the most?

☐ Physical   ☐ Emotional

☐ Mental   ☐ Relational

☐ Spiritual   ☐ Financial

Why?_____

_____

_____

_____

_____

_____

I will put my *One Word* **into action by:**

_____

_____

_____

_____

_____

_____

_____

I will **impact others** with my *One Word* by:

_____

_____

_____

_____

_____

_____

_____

WEEKLY EXPERIENCE

Lessons and insights I learned this week **living my *One Word*:**

_____
_____
_____
_____
_____
_____
_____
_____
_____
_____
_____
_____
_____
_____

The blessings and challenges of living my *One Word*:

_____

_____

_____

_____

_____

_____

_____

_____

WEEKLY WIN

_____

_____

_____

_____

_____

WEEKLY FOCUS
GIVE THANKS

Gratitude is powerful. It strengthens relation-ships. It improves mental health. It lifts spirits. Be intentional and find gratitude for your One Word Journey and stretch team.

What areas need my *One Word* the most?

☐ Physical   ☐ Emotional

☐ Mental   ☐ Relational

☐ Spiritual   ☐ Financial

Why?_____

_____

_____

_____

_____

_____

_____

I will put my *One Word* into action by:

_____

_____

_____

_____

_____

_____

I will **impact others** with my *One Word*
by:

_____

_____

_____

_____

_____

_____

WEEKLY EXPERIENCE

Lessons and insights I learned this week living my *One Word*:

_____

_____

_____

_____

_____

_____

_____

_____

_____

_____

_____

_____

_____

_____

_____

_____

The **blessings and challenges** of living my *One Word*:

_____

_____

_____

_____

_____

_____

_____

_____

WEEKLY WIN

_____

_____

_____

_____

_____

WEEKLY FOCUS
LEAVE A LEGACY

At the end of your life, what do you hope people say about you? What mark do you want to leave on this world? Consider how your One Word can help you leave a legacy.

What areas need my *One Word* the most?

☐ Physical   ☐ Emotional

☐ Mental   ☐ Relational

☐ Spiritual   ☐ Financial

Why?_____
_____
_____
_____
_____
_____
_____

I will put my *One Word* **into action by:**

_____

_____

_____

_____

_____

_____

_____

I will **impact others** with my *One Word* by:

_____

_____

_____

_____

_____

_____

_____

WEEKLY EXPERIENCE

Lessons and insights I learned this week **living my *One Word*:**

_____

_____

_____

_____

_____

_____

_____

_____

_____

_____

_____

_____

_____

_____

_____

_____

The **blessings and challenges** of
living my *One Word*:

_____

_____

_____

_____

_____

_____

_____

_____

WEEKLY WIN

_____

_____

_____

_____

_____

_____

"Standing between two years is a good place to evaluate our lives. Looking back, we remember the year that has passed—its delights and disappointments fresh in our memories. Looking around, we see clearly where we are—able to make good choices based on our actual circumstances. And looking ahead, we anticipate another twelve months that hold the possibilities of high hopes and new dreams."

Chuck Swindoll

Annual Review

Even though the year is over, your *One Word* Journey is not something to check off a to-do list and put behind you. If you have lived your word for 365 days, your year was probably a journey of ups and downs that have shaped you into the person you were created to be. Remember: You don't conquer or master your word. Rather, you learn and experience what your *One Word* brings. The *One Word* Journey is about focusing and simplifying so you can experience greater meaning, mission, passion, and purpose.

It is invaluable to take time to stop and reflect on your *One Word* Journey. We believe it's important to review how your *One Word* has developed you. Take time now to reflect over your past year.

How has your life changed because of your *One Word*?

_____

_____

_____

_____

_____

_____

_____

_____

_____

What lessons did you learn this past year as a result of your *One Word*?

_____

_____

_____

_____

_____

_____

_____

_____

_____

What were the blessings?

_____

_____

_____

_____

_____

_____

_____

_____

What were the challenges?

_____

_____

_____

_____

_____

_____

_____

_____

What is one example of something you did differently as a result of your word?

_____

_____

_____

_____

_____

_____

_____

_____

How did your word impact those around you? Family? Workplace? Friends?

_____

_____

_____

_____

_____

_____

_____

_____

_____

How did your stretch team help you with your word?

_____

_____

_____

_____

_____

_____

_____

If you could summarize your *One Word* into one sentence, what would you say?

_____

_____

_____

_____

_____

_____

_____

_____

_____

Make sure to take time to enjoy and celebrate that you've made it to the end of your
One Word Journey. Be sure to take what
you learned this past year into next year;
don't let the life-changes leave you. It's
never too early to start planning for your
next *One Word*.

What's one thing you can do to celebrate
how your *One Word* impacted you?

_____

_____

_____

_____

_____

_____

_____

_____

Access additional *One Word* resources, make your own *One Word* poster, and more at www.Getoneword.com.

THREE TIPS FOR CHOOSING YOUR *ONE WORD*

1. **Discover, Don't Pick:** Many times people say they picked their *One Word* instead of discovering a word. Over the years, I have learned my word finds me if I am willing to be patient and silent. There is a word meant for you.

2. **Don't Stress:** We drift to complexity instead of driving to simplicity. *One Word* is a simple discipline that is not difficult. Too many people feel like there is a perfect word and it is their job to find it, like trying to find a needle in a haystack. Stress less and have fun with it. There are probably many words for you each year; identifying your *One Word* is part of the journey. Remember: You will have many more years for more words. Every year's word is another chapter in your story.

3. **Honor the Process:** Don't rush into the year and bypass the three-step process of

Looking In, Looking Up, and Looking Out.
There is power in this process. When I have
honored the process and taken the time to
do it properly, I have discovered a word that
is different from the one I originally thought
would define my year.

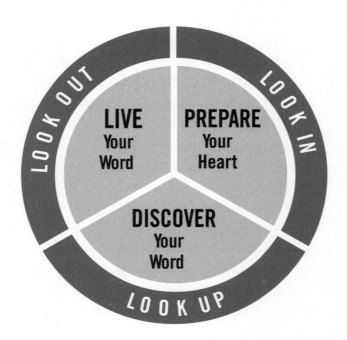

52 WEEKLY TIPS

1. **Renew Your Faith**

   You are not an accident. You have a purpose. As you start your *One Word* journey pray for wisdom and insight. Renew your faith and trust in God's bigger plan for your life

2. **Pay Attention**

   Intentionality with your *One Word* will open your eyes and heart to see what you've missed before now. Pay attention to what you see.

3. **Embrace the Struggle**

   Pain is not meaningless. Every struggle comes with purpose. Apply your *One Word* to the areas that are bringing you the most stress this week.

4. **Character Counts**

   How often do you stop to reflect on your character? Where is it strong? Where do you need to develop? Look for how your *One Word* plays a role.

5. **Make a Difference**

   You were made to make a difference in this world—to leave it a little better than you found it. There is purpose for your life. Your *One Word* will help reveal it.

6. **Find a Cause**

   A cause is something bigger than yourself. Joining a cause can bring passion, purpose, and meaning. Reflect on what causes your *One Word* is leading you to.

7. **Fight Discouragement**

   Negativity and pessimistic thoughts often bombard us, and they lead to discouragement. Use your *One Word* to fight this, and instead find encouragement.

8. **Believe You Can**

   A "can do" spirit accomplishes anything. Positivity helps you make forward progress. Consider how your *One Word* can help you say yes this week.

9. **Cut Distractions**

   Notifications, pings, and dings are relentless; they can interrupt us when we're on a roll. How can you remove distractions and focus on your *One Word*?

10. Celebrate

Life is full of things worth celebrating. From special occasions to small wins, celebrations make life full. How can your *One Word* help you celebrate?

11. Find Small Wins

Always build in ways to pause, review your incremental progress, and appreciate how far you've come. Find joy by acknowledging your small wins.

12. Connect to Keep Going

Everyone gets discouraged and needs connection to snap out of it. Pick someone in your inner circle and share your *One Word* progress so far.

13. Check In

Don't overestimate the power of your stretch team. They can help you keep your *One Word* goals on track. Check in with them to share how it's going.

14. Monitor for Burnout

A fast pace can lead to burnout and discouragement. Your *One Word* will bring you life. In what areas are you feeling burned out? Make a plan to go slower.

15. **Remember Your "Why"**

Why did you choose your *One Word*? What motivated you to dive into this journey? Remember your "why" to find momentum to keep going.

16. **Keep It Fresh**

Find someone new with whom to share your *One Word*, someone who hasn't heard it before. Tell them why you chose it and the impact it's made on your life so far.

17. **Define Success**

Some say success is winning over losing. Some say it's completion. Some say it's doing the right things consistently over time. How do you define it?

18. **Be Consistent**

Starts and stops threaten to derail progress. Doing the little things every day to pursue your *One Word* will create the results you want.

19. **Take Action**

It's one thing to think up a plan; it's another to take action. Your *One Word* Journey requires action. Don't just think this week—do.

20. **Front and Center**

What reminder systems work for you and help you keep things front and center each morning? Set up a way for your *One Word* to be front and center.

21. **Find the Inch**

"Inch by inch, life's a cinch. Yard by yard, life's hard." In what ways have you made inches of progress in your *One Word* Journey so far? Find and celebrate.

22. **Focus on Now**

There's nothing worse than feeling stuck, like nothing positive is happening. But sometimes you're looking too far ahead. Focus on what's happening today.

23. **Step Each Step**

Temptation tells us to skip steps on the *One Word* Journey and bypass challenges and hard work. But to get the results you want, don't miss a step.

24. **Look for Opportunities**

If you pray for patience, God won't automatically make you patient; He will give you opportunities to grow. Consider the opportunities before you this week.

25. **Process over Problems**

    Life brings potholes and speed bumps, but progress is a process. Let your *One Word* help you focus on the person you are becoming over the problems.

26. **Do Not Disturb**

    Without intentionally setting aside time to focus on your *One Word* Journey, you will miss it. Set aside time where you can't be disturbed so you can truly reflect.

27. **Keep Going**

    Demand and perseverance on the front-end leads to big-time payoffs in the end. If you're in the middle, don't quit. Let your *One Word* keep you focused.

28. **Expect the Unexpected**

    Don't be someone who says, "I didn't see that coming." Expect the unexpected. Even if you have an idea about how *One Word* will turn out, be open to surprise.

29. **In Plain Sight**

    "Out of sight, out of mind." It's a common phrase, but it's true. Remember your *One Word* this week and put it in plain sight. Make sure you won't miss it.

30. **Press Pause**

Are you going so fast that you're missing what matters most to you? It's time to press pause and slow down. Be present and reflect over your *One Word*.

31. **Slow Down**

Are you addicted to busyness? Did you know it will distract you and put you on overdrive? What's one less thing you can do this week?

32. **Be Present**

Your journey has a beginning and an end. It's good to remember the goal. But don't forget to be present. How is your *One Word* impacting your life right now?

33. **Share with Others**

Telling others about your *One Word* Journey will bless them and reinvigorate you. Sharing benefits others and creates momentum. Share this week.

34. **Better Together**

One Word doesn't benefit only you; it can also benefit the groups you're in. How can your family, friends, team, and other groups benefit from your *One Word*?

35. **Build Chemistry**

Build unity and trust with teams, companies, and families by choosing a *One Word* together. It will become a rallying cry and keep you focused on your mission.

36. **Talk about It**

Conversations about your *One Word* will both help you and help others. Share your big wins. Share your small wins. Ask for help. Talk about it.

37. **Bless Others**

As we become our best, we are better to others. Let *One Word* change you and make you more focused on serving and blessing others in your life.

38. **Discover**

Do you feel like your *One Word* picked you, rather than you picked it? A lot of people do. There's a reason why it's for you this year. Discover it.

39. **Progress Not Perfection**

Too many people feel like there is a perfect world, and the *One Word* Journey will be perfect. There is no such thing. There will be hills and valleys. Pursue progress, not perfection.

40. **Grow versus Conquer**

Everybody loves winning, but *One Word* isn't about winning or conquering. Take inventory on how your *One Word* is helping you grow through success and failure.

41. **Don't Look Back**

Disappointment and fatigue may cause you to want a "redo." Don't give in. Keep moving forward and trust your process. Take steps forward, not back.

42. **Don't Compare**

Your *One Word* Journey is unique to you. Don't compare it with others, and don't compare it with past years. Focus on the present year, on today.

43. **Make a Difference**

When your *One Word* infiltrates every area of your life, you'll find that the people around you will benefit too. Let your *One Word* help those you serve.

44. **Enjoy the Journey**

One Word is meant to be fun. It's meant to be life-changing. While it may get hard and challenging at some points, find the positives and enjoy it.

45. Hidden Treasures

You may be surprised at the ways *One Word* is showing up. It's normal if you thought you'd see change in one area, only to find it somewhere else. Keep going.

46. Keep It Simple

One Word is designed to be a simple way to experience life transformation. It's not meant to be complicated, and it doesn't need to be. Resist complexity.

47. Say No

Boundaries: Do you have them? Your *One Word* is a guide for your year, and to follow it you'll likely need to say no so you can stay on track. Practice it. Boundaries are worth it.

48. The Answer

One Word is a guiding light for your year. Faced with decisions and trying to discern which way to go? Consider how your *One Word* may be leading to your answer.

49. Push Yourself

The *One Word* Journey won't be comfortable; change creates tension, but tension leads to growth. In what ways are you challenged to push yourself to become a better you?

50. Say Yes

How does fear hold you back? What dreams have yet to become a reality? Consider how your *One Word* is leading you to say yes to what's previously been a no.

51. Give Thanks

Gratitude is powerful. It strengthens relationships. It improves mental health. It lifts spirits. Be intentional and find gratitude for your *One Word* Journey and stretch team.

52. Leave a Legacy

At the end of your life, what do you hope people say about you? What mark do you want to leave on this world? Consider how your *One Word* can help you leave a legacy.

Your Weekly Wins

1.

2.

3.

4.

5.

6.

7.

8.

9.

10.

11.

12.

13.

14.

15.

16.

17.

18.

19.

20.

21.

22.

23.

24.

25.

26.

27.

28.

29.

30.

31.

32.

33.

34.

35.

36.

37.

38.

39.

40.

41.

42.

43.

44.

45.

46.

47.

48.

49.

50.

51.

52.

"Start by doing what's necessary, then do what's possible, and suddenly you're doing the impossible."

St. Francis of Assisi

Additional *One Word* Resources

Source: © Alex Slobodkin/Getty Images

GetOneWord.com

The power of *One Word* has already changed thousands of lives. Now it's your turn. We have produced free resources to help you do that. These resources will help you put the *One Word* process into practice.

- Share your *One Word* story.
- Download your free *One Word* Action Plan.
- Create and share *One Word* posters.
- Watch the *One Word* video.
- Sign up for our free newsletter.
- Discover creative *One Word* reminders.

One Word That Will Change Your Team

If you are interested in taking your leadership team or organization through the *One Word* process, we conduct leadership retreats, training, and team-building sessions for all types of organizations. Following is our contact information.

E-mail: info@GetOneWord.com

Online: GetOneWord.com

Free monthly newsletter: GetOneWord.com

Twitter: @GetOneWord

Facebook: Facebook.com/GetOneWord

About the Authors

Jon Gordon has inspired millions of readers around the world. He is the author of 27 books, including five children's books and thirteen best-sellers: *The Energy Bus, The Carpenter, Training Camp, You Win in the Locker Room First, The Power of Positive Leadership, The Power of a Positive Team, The Coffee Bean, Stay Positive, The Garden, Relationship Grit, Stick Together, Row the Boat,* and *The Sale*. He is passionate about developing positive leaders, organizations, and teams. Visit him at **JonGordon.com**

Dan Britton is a speaker, writer, coach, and trainer whose mission is to help people pursue their passion. He serves as the Chief Field Officer with the Fellowship of Christian Athletes where he has been on staff since 1990. Dan travels extensively around the world training thousands of leaders in over 100 countries. He played professional lacrosse with the Baltimore Thunder, earning a spot on the All-Star team, and was nominated by his teammates for both the Service and Unsung Hero awards. Dan has coauthored eight books including *One Word*, *Wisdom Walks*, *True Competitor*, and *Wisdom Challenge*. Additionally, he has authored and edited twelve books with the Fellowship of Christian Athletes. Dan is a frequent speaker for companies, nonprofits, sports teams, schools, and churches. He has been interviewed by national outlets like FOX News, CBS News, and Fast Company. He still plays and coaches lacrosse and enjoys running marathons, even completing the Boston Marathon twice. Dan and his wife, Dawn, reside in Overland Park, Kansas, and have three adult married children: Kallie, Abby, and Elijah. You can e-mail Dan at **dan@fca.org**. Follow him on social **@fcadan**.

Jimmy Page is the Founder and President of the Unstoppable Freedom Alliance and the Be Unstoppable life & leadership system. He's an entrepreneur, health & wellness expert, Spartan athlete, podcaster, and high-performance coach. Jimmy is the author of several books including *One Word, True Competitor, WisdomWalks, Life Word, Called to Greatness, One Word for Kids*, and more. He's a frequent speaker for conferences, events, schools, sports teams, churches, and businesses in every industry including the *NFL, NCAA, YMCA, Intel, Salvation Army, State Farm*, and many more. Jimmy is a husband and proud father of four grown kids. He and his wife started a cancer foundation called Believe Big following her victory over cancer. His mission is to inspire you to live the unstoppable life – unleashing your best in every way. Visit his website at beunstoppable.live or email him at **Jimmy@beunstoppable.live**.